Martha Reeves

Weave Leno

In-Depth Instructions for All Levels, with 7 Projects

Schiffer Publishing Ltd
4880 Lower Valley Road • Atglen, PA 19310

Designed by RoS
Cover design by Brenda McCallum
All weaving, sewing, and sketches by the author
Type set in GoudySans BT/GoudyOlSt BT

ISBN: 978-0-7643-5101-3
Printed in China

Published by Schiffer Publishing, Ltd.
4880 Lower Valley Road
Atglen, PA 19310
Phone: (610) 593-1777; Fax: (610) 593-2002
E-mail: Info@schifferbooks.com
Web: www.schifferbooks.com

For our complete selection of fine books on this and related subjects, please visit our website at www.schifferbooks.com. You may also write for a free catalog.

Schiffer Publishing's titles are available at special discounts for bulk purchases for sales promotions or premiums. Special editions, including personalized covers, corporate imprints, and excerpts, can be created in large quantities for special needs. For more information, contact the publisher.

We are always looking for people to write books on new and related subjects. If you have an idea for a book, please contact us at proposals@schifferbooks.com.

Other Schiffer Books on Related Subjects:

The Art of Weaving, Else Regensteiner, afterword by Margie Thompson, ISBN 978-0-7643-4856-3

Weaving Shaker Rugs: Traditional Techniques to Create Beautiful Reproduction Rugs and Tapes, Mary Elva Congleton Erf, ISBN 978-0-7643-4907-2

Norwegian Pick-Up Bandweaving, Heather Torgenrud, ISBN 978-0-7643-4751-1

Contents

acknowledgments

I wish to thank the weavers, who before me researched the lenos, Berta Frey, Mary Atwater, and Kathryn Wertenberger to name just a few. Their early exploration of the lenos set the ground work and led us to where we are today.

This book would not have come about without my family's loving encouragement. Most of all I thank my dear husband for his belief in me and taking over the cooking and grocery shopping to allow me more time for weaving and writing. I also wish to thank my family and friends for their understanding when I was absent from so many functions. I could not have done it without their understanding support.

Weavers who understand what I do were also great encouragers. When I came up against roadblocks, they urged me to go on. I wish to especially thank one of my colleagues, Chris Jeryan, who helped me get started with this book.

preface

When working on the Certificate of Excellence (COE), an expertise program adminstered by Handweavers Guild of America, Inc., I came to the required loom-controlled leno portion of study. As I began researching this technique I was immediately fascinated by the process. As I found myself delving deeper into the study, a new energy and excitement was generated. Who would have thought that one could make parallel warp threads cross and twist around each other? It is truly a magical and mysterious weave.

My hope is that you will find the same excitement and passion as you progress through this book. You will find both loom-controlled leno and finger-manipulated leno methods explained, with easy-to-follow instructions for the processes. I urge you to take the time to work through the seven projects presented here, taking your leno skills to your next level.

1. HISTORY

The history of textiles began over 2,000 years ago.

We are fortunate that weavers have access to the many historic resources

from early times in museum collections. We have much to learn

from our rich heritage.

Due to the drier lands in many countries, preserved textiles have been found sealed in tombs and in clay jars. Among the excavated textiles, gauze that is approximately 2,000 years old was found in the tombs of some members of the nobility.

The forerunner of the leno weaving technique was gauze. Gauze, meaning a weave with crossed warps, breaks all the rules that weavers have practiced for centuries. The rule was to have a fixed warp with all the threads parallel to each other. This was maintained throughout the weaving process. This principle is not followed in gauze or leno. Warp threads actually cross over one another and are locked in place by the weft.

Triple lozenge design, silk gauze, Han Dynasty, 206 BCE–220 CE. *Courtesy of Philadelphia Museum of Art, Philadelphia, Pennsylvania. Purchased with the Bloomfield Moore Fund.*

∽ Early Gauze Weaving ∽

Gauze is seen as a light or sheer cloth; it is usually of one color. Many gauzes were woven in silk with a single weft, adding to its delicate structure. It is debatable where the gauze weaving technique first began. Irene Emery states in *The Primary Structures of Fabrics* (1966) that the term *gauze* was named for the city of Gaza in Palestine, so we assume it was woven in that region. We know Gaza was a city of active commerce, trading and exporting textiles as well as other commodities.

When a special decorative cloth was required for royalty, the gauze was woven with linen. Gauze weaving was achieved by twisting the warp threads with the fingers, a very time-consuming process.

The early looms were nothing like today's shaft looms. One of the early upright looms had a rock-weighted warp. The vertical loom required that the weaver stand to weave (Figure 1-1). In Israel the Bedouin people, nomads, wove on horizontal looms which had short legs they planted into the ground to hold it firm (Figure 1-2). When it was time to move their camp, they simply pulled up the stakes, rolled up the warp, and moved on.

Figure 1-1. Early Egyptian loom. (Drawing inspired by Joan Weaver)

Recent excavations in Northern China have revealed many textiles. Among them are gauzes. The Han Dynasty period (around 206 BCE to 220 CE) is very important for textile historians due to the advanced skills its artifacts represent. John Becker tells of the discovery of gauze textiles in *Pattern and Loom* (1987). A patterned silk executed in gauze was found in the Mawangdui Tomb No. 1 (168 BCE). A similar embroidered gauze garment was found in a tomb in Hubei dated 300 BCE. All of these gauzes are believed to be hand-manipulated gauze cloth entirely woven in twisted warp threads.

Gauze was especially prevalent in ancient Peru, as far back as the second millennium BCE. According to Becker, one of the often-found characteristics of Peruvian gauze is larger, uneven open spaces of untwisted warp. The open spaces for the design were used in more complex textiles, where a delicate web-like appearance was desired. Their simple gauze was woven with fine over-twisted cotton, giving the finished piece a crepe-like appearance. The Peruvian method of weaving gauze, according to John Becker, appears to be very complicated but is really quite simple. The weaver twined the weft around groups of warp threads. When the row was finished the weft was pulled straight, thus twisting the warp. When weaving patterned gauze, two wefts were used, each with their own purpose, pattern, and background. At that time the early Peruvians wove on a simple body tension loom, called a back strap loom.

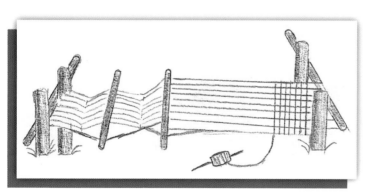

Figure 1-2. Early horizontal loom. (Drawing inspired by Joan Weaver)

Leno Beginnings

From gauze, we come to leno, pronounced *'lē no*, which was once called "fancy gauze." Emery defines the term *leno* as twisted warps with a doubled or heavier weft thread than that of gauze. The term was derived from the French word *linon* (itself derived from the name of the French city Laon), meaning a cross-woven or gauze-woven lawn. In earlier times cloth was woven in the leno technique in narrow strips, usually with cotton. Emery cites the word *gauze* as being more useful as a designation for a crossed-warp type of weave than the term *leno*. Leno resembles gauze but has areas of gauze separated with areas of plain or basket weave. Leno is recognized by the characteristic two threads up, two threads down for each twist.

The leno weaving technique spread to other countries, each giving it their own unique style. In fact it is hard to find a country where leno was not woven. Becker writes about a leno from the 1500s in Finland, known as Karelian lace, which was used for borders and decorative motifs. In Eastern Europe the leno techniques were created as a result of experimentation. In Denmark, tablecloths woven with decorative borders of leno were also the result of experimentation. We often see complicated leno designs from Belgium woven in "figured leno" and used for curtains of ecru cotton. The Romanians created leno textiles with figured designs such as flowers and leaves.

Tarascan Lace

Tarascan lace, another type of leno, originated in Morelia, Mexico. No two authors agree on the origin of this leno. The history of Morelia, Mexico, written for Berea College by Margarita Graetzer (2011), states that the Tarascan Indians, also called the Tarascos, migrated from Peru to central Mexico before the 1300s. They created their own patterns of leno with a Peruvian influence. Wayne Anderson, reporter and professor, chronicled in his blog, *Venture Bound*, that the cultural dominance of the Aztecs followed by the Spaniards in Mexico could have had an influence on their crafts.

Whichever it was, the Tarascos developed unique designs in their weaving, which is easily recognized as theirs alone. The dominant pattern is the diagonal designs, which are made up of 2- and 4-thread hand-manipulated leno. The women wove the beautiful leno on back strap looms and called their textiles Tarascan lace. There are a few weavers remaining in Mexico who are still weaving Tarascan lace. However, other students of the technique have carried on the familiar weave. One of those persons was Gladys Smith of Vallejo, California. Many of her textiles were donated to the Thousand Islands Art Center, Home of the Handweaving Museum, located in Clayton, New York.

⤫ Chenille ⤬

We know chenille today as a fuzzy soft yarn. Early chenille thread was actually created from a woven cloth. Clinton Gilroy describes the then-new technique in his book *The Art of Weaving by Hand and Power* (1844) as "weaving chenille thread." Gilroy writes that in 1820, textile producer Alexander Buchannan needed a method of creating shawls with varying colors throughout the yarn. Buchannan used a simple leno technique, with a strong fine warp that was widely spaced on the loom and woven with a weft of many colors. When the fabric came off the loom, it was cut lengthwise between the twisted warps, resulting in a furry yarn to be used for his shawls.

⤫ Early Chinese Weavers ⤬

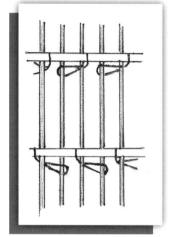

Figure 1-3. Early doup stick, a tool to weave gauze.

The Chinese may not have been the first to use the doup method of weaving leno, but they have left us the first known recorded example of it. We know the craftsmen were paid by the finished product, according to John Becker. There was no time for hand manipulation of threads for gauze weaving if the workers were to make a living wage. In their resourcefulness, they created a loom-controlled "doup method" of gauze weaving. This method greatly increased the speed of their weaving. The early method involved tying looped strings first around a warp thread then onto a doup stick, as in Figure 1-3, which was raised to pull the neighboring thread across to weave a twist. Harriet Tidball simplified the doup technique in 1957 in *The Handloom Weaves*. She clearly describes by picture and description how to tie and thread the doups for our modern shaft looms.

⤫ New Leno Techniques ⤬

New leno techniques were studied as the harness looms became popular. In *Treatise on The Art of Weaving* (1845), John Murphy explored all the leno and gauze techniques available at that time. His methods seem primitive compared to today's methods. He devised "half leaves" (doups), a tool to weave loom-controlled leno, as seen in Figure 1-4. Even though we find the old terminology hard to understand, we have to appreciate his work to bring technology to the modern weavers using harness looms. Today's method of weaving leno is not that different.

Murphy also introduced the use of a glass bead as a tool for weaving leno. This was the first time a weaver experimented with beads as a tool to twist the warp thread in a loom-controlled leno. He suggested the weaver proceed slowly to allow threads to pass each other "in the reed slot thus preventing bead tangles."

Bead leno had not been woven frequently prior to that point, but as time went by, weavers worked to improve on his method. Bead leno began to be seen more after William Watson published a full description of the "bead mounting," or bead leno, in 1947 in his book *Advanced Textile Design*. Here he touts bead leno as being "cheaper" than doup leno. Cost was an important factor in the 1940s.

The old writings were studied by weaver Mary Atwater. She put a lot of effort into creating an easier method of weaving doup leno. She began publishing her findings from her experimentation with the doup technique in 1936, with her article "Peruvian Leno" in *The Weaver*. She also tested ways to weave bead leno. In addition to the beads she devised a "release mechanism," sometimes called a "release frame." This mechanism appears in her article "The Bead-Leno Weave" in *Practical Weaving Suggestions* (1950). It is described as two dowels separated by six inches, forming a frame. The frame was laid within the warp threads, resting on the beaded threads, positioned between the back beam and the shafts. It acted as a weight to hold floating warp threads in place. Atwater removed the mystery of weaving bead leno for weavers today with her clear instructions in her publication *American Hand-Weaving* (1973). Atwater focuses on the doup method of weaving leno but is equally well versed in the bead method, and her work calmed the fears of many who hesitated to try weaving leno.

One of the most disputed of tools has been the bead. The bead is threaded onto two of the warp threads in the twisting unit, as the threads come from the heddles and before being threaded through the reed. Many weavers have recommended "the perfect" bead. Small segments of drinking straws were used by Atwater, Alderman, Sullivan, and Wertenberger. Oval or tubular beads or even pearls were used by Atwater, as well. Sullivan also suggests that quarter-inch grommets would make a good bead. Today we have many choices of beads available, and recently, well-known weavers have written about bead leno.

From gauze, to doup, to bead leno, throughout time the leno weaving techniques have developed into those that we have—and enjoy—today.

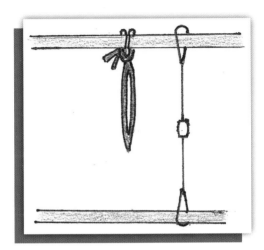

Figure 1-4. Doup, a tool used for weaving doup leno.

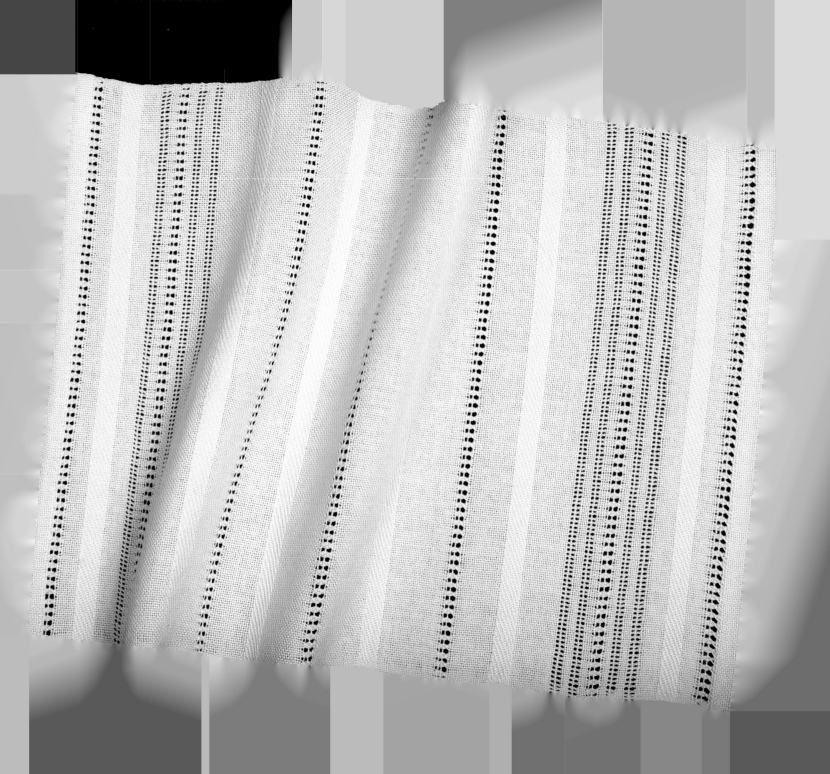

2. PICK UP LENO

Pick up leno, also known as finger-manipulated leno, is one of the easiest lenos to weave. The main advantage in weaving leno in a finger-manipulated manner is its simplicity. Perhaps you were introduced to it in a beginning weaving class. Both new and seasoned weavers will enjoy the excitement of leno.

Much creativity and skill goes into each piece, where pattern possibilities are endless. The twist in the warp renders the cloth stable and very practical for any use, even though there are lacy openings in the cloth. Woven with the correct beat, a sleazy cloth can be avoided.

Pick up leno is in the plain weave class of weaving and is actually a weaving technique, not a weave. The base structure is typically plain weave. However, it can easily be combined with any other weave structure. With finger-manipulated leno the weaver can select where to place the twists. There are hundreds of variations, too many to list. You may incorporate many types of leno within one piece. One possible use is as a border for summer and winter placemats, or as a division between pieces on a warp.

The loom set up is the same as plain weave for basic lace effects. Pick up leno does not weave up quickly. Each and every twist requires the weaver's fingers to pick and manipulate every leno twist across the width of the warp, thus requiring a patient weaver.

Weaving Successful Pick Up Leno

Tools

Generally, the lenos are woven on a two- or four-harness loom. The loom may be any loom that can produce plain weave.

A sturdy pick-up stick or sword is required. The stick should be 1.5" wide with a slight point at one end. The length needs to be at least as long as your warp is wide.

The shuttle must be the thinnest you have to avoid friction on the warp threads. A maximum 1.5" in height is required to slide through the shed, which is forced by the pick-up stick. The stick shuttles work best.

As with all lenos, the warp has a tendency to draw in. To overcome this inclination, use a temple and move it often.

Standard Threading and Tie-up

A plain weave threading is used for most lenos. However, some lenos included here use another threading. A two-shaft loom is threaded with the yarn on shaft 1, followed by yarn on shaft 2, repeating across all warp threads. For a multi-shaft loom, thread a straight draw as in plain weave. Example: thread shaft 1, then shaft 2, followed by shaft 3 and 4, repeat. Tie up the warp with a light to medium warp tension. The treadle tie-up is the same as for plain weave. Tie up one treadle with yarns on shafts 1 and 3, then shafts 2 and 4 on the next treadle.

Yarns

The twisting warp ends are under considerable tension while weaving, so strong smooth warp yarns are recommended. Mercerized cotton and plied smooth linens are among the best. These yarns will better define the open lacy areas. Soft or textured yarns will weave just fine; however, they will fill in and close the lacy spaces.

Except for special effects the weft is the same yarn as the warp, sometimes used singly. A creative touch can be achieved using different colors. Using yarns of slight color or value difference gives a more textural effect. Experiment however you like, but it is generally accepted that leno is most effective when woven in a single color.

Design

There are many variations in pick up leno. Some are created by the warp spacing, others by the technique. Many lenos are more textural. The sett works hand in hand with the yarn size and is generally the same as for plain weave. A loose sett with 8/2 yarns would be sett at 16 to 18 epi. Additionally, lacy effects are achieved by skipping dents. Try threading the reed 1-2-3-4, skip two dents or more, and repeat. The 1/1 leno gives a finer look with not as many open areas. The more warp ends in the picked up twists, the bolder and more interesting the design.

When the leno twists are the same in each row, the open spaces occur in columns, one above the other. Offsetting the pick up on successive rows creates a diagonal design. Leno worked on a closed shed is tighter, bolder, and more precise. A single or double weft may be used.

It is best to design your pattern first on graph paper. Keep in mind the planned open space is your goal for designs that are visually more appealing. Use your imagination, combining and offsetting the leno. Many designs have been named.

✓ Tips for Successful Pick Up Leno

1. Thread the loom and tie up the treadles as for plain weave, unless otherwise specified.

2. For most lenos the first thread at the right edge must be from the top shed when the treadle is pressed. This is very important.

3. Spread the warp by weaving a plain weave header or a planned hem.

4. Use moderate warp tension. If it is difficult to get the pick-up stick through, release the warp tension slightly.

5. Use a temple and angle the weft, to avoid draw-in.

6. Begin the leno pattern row at the right selvage.

7. When all twists are picked up on the pick-up stick, turn on edge and check for errors. Send the shuttle through the shed.

8. Remove the pick-up stick and beat firmly for a stronger cloth. A lighter touch will result in a more sheer and delicate texture.

9. Following the pattern row, return the shuttle to the right by pressing the next treadle to weave a tabby return. The twisted warp threads are now returned to a neutral position.

❧ Pick Up Leno Variations ❧

1/1 Leno

1/1 leno is a fine open-shed leno which is also known as Antique Mexican Singles.

Use the standard threading and tie-up. To achieve this pattern, press treadle one. Beginning at the right, pull the first raised warp to the left with the fingers of the left hand. With the right hand, pick up the lower thread and guide it onto the pick-up stick. Let the upper thread fall under the pick-up stick. Continue across the warp, picking up the next lower thread and let the next upper thread drop, keeping all the twisted threads on the pick-up stick. Close the shed. Slide the shuttle through the shed created by the pick-up stick. Follow the tips listed previously to complete this leno.

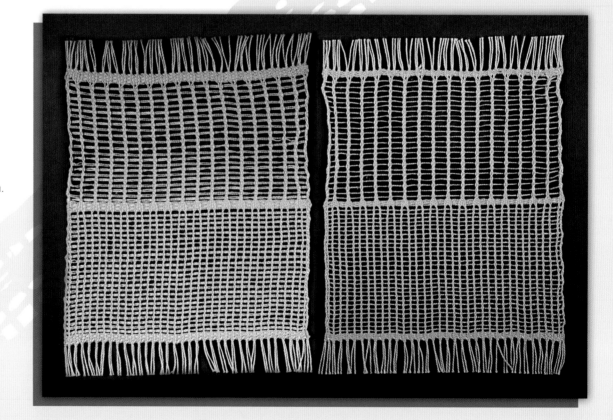

Left 1/1 leno. Right 2/2 leno.
Doubled weft in lower portion.

2/2 Leno

The 2/2 leno, also known as Antique Mexican Doubles, is slightly more coarse than the 1/1 leno.

Thread the loom in a straight draw and use the standard threading and tie-up. The open areas are more pronounced as this leno offers a more lacy effect. However, the more open lenos have a greater tendency to draw in. Use a temple to maintain good selvages. Work from the right, pressing treadle 1 to raise the first right selvage thread. Draw the upper threads left with the left hand. Pick up the next two lower threads onto the pick-up stick. Let the upper two threads drop under the pick-up stick. Continue across the warp in this manner. Throw the shuttle as described. Separate the twisted rows by pressing treadle 2 for a tabby return.

Leno Spots

If a nice texture with fewer open spaces is what you want, weave leno spots.

Leno spots are woven on an open shed. Use the standard threading and tie-up. Press treadle 1 and pass the pick-up stick under the first three upper threads. Make a single 1/1 leno twist by picking up one lower thread and dropping one upper thread under the pick-up stick. Continue in this manner across the warp. Change to treadle 2 and tabby back. On the next pattern row, slip the pick-up stick under the first two upper threads, and make a 1/1 leno twist offsetting the design. Then continue as before slipping the shuttle under three threads then forming a 1/1 twist. Return the shuttle right while pressing treadle 2. In the third pattern row, slip the shuttle under only one upper thread then make the twist as before as you continue across the row. Press treadle 2 and return the shuttle right. This completes one pattern sequence.

Leno spots.

Peruvian Gauze Doubles

This is a 2/2 closed-shed leno. Peruvian doubles are a tighter yet more open leno. Use the standard threading and treadle tie-up. Pull the first two warp threads left while picking up the next two threads onto the pick-up stick. Drop the next two threads under the pick-up stick. When the row is completed, beat firmly to place the twists. Press treadle 2 and tabby back.

Milwaukee Lace

Milwaukee lace has a lacy effect yet it has fewer open spaces. It is woven with the shed open, twisting only the upper threads and ignoring all lower threads. Use the standard threading and tie-up. Press treadle 1 and work right to left. Create a single twist in the upper threads only. Pull the first upper thread left while the second thread is pulled right and onto the pick-up stick. Let the first upper thread fall under the pick-up stick. Continue in this manner across the warp. Follow with three tabby shots.

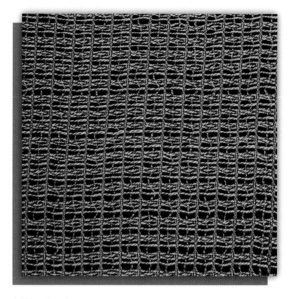

Milwaukee lace.

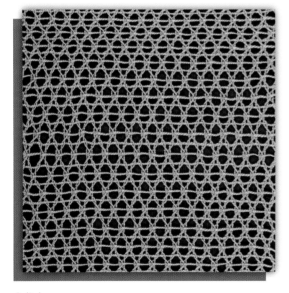

Split leno.

Split Leno

The 2/2 split leno forms a pattern of diamond or circular open shapes, resulting from the splitting of the pairs on succeeding rows.

Use the standard threading and treadle tie-up. Work the first row of leno on an open shed, pressing treadle 1 and picking up 2/2 leno. Return the weft to the right selvage pressing treadle 2. For the second pattern row, begin and end with a single 1/1 leno, picking up the 2/2 leno as before throughout the middle portion. Notice that the second leno row contains a top and a bottom warp thread from two of the previous rows of twists. Just as before, press treadle 2 and return the shuttle with a tabby shot. Alternate these two pattern rows to form the design you desire. A zigzag effect can be seen in the patterning between rows.

Mexican Doubles

This wide-open leno is very lacy. Throughout the cloth there is a distinctive corded effect. Use this technique when warp emphasis along with good selvages are important.

The total warp ends must be a multiple of four, then adding two. An example would be 38 or 50 warp threads. Use the standard threading and tie-up. Beginning at the right selvage and with treadle 1 pressed, pick up three threads from the lower shed and let the next two upper threads drop under the pick-up stick. Next, pick up two and let two drop. Repeat the 2/2 leno working to the left. For the last twist, pick up two and let three drop under the pick-up stick. Beat firmly. Return the shuttle to the right by pressing treadle 2 to tabby back.

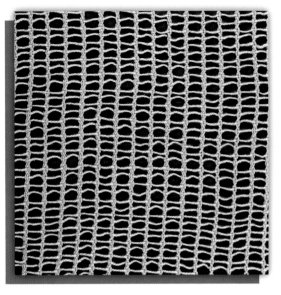

Mexican doubles.

Alternate Gauze

Curves of laciness and open-textured weave are created by combining plain weave with a simple 3/3 leno. Use the standard threading and treadle tie-up. With the shed closed, pull the first three threads left while picking up the next three threads onto the pick-up stick. Press treadle 1 and slide the pick-up stick into the shed under the next three top threads, as in plain weave. Form the next 3/3 leno as before. Continue in this manner across the warp. Follow the leno row with three plain weave rows. On the next pattern row, begin with plain weave under three warps followed by 3/3 leno, offsetting the design from the previous pattern row. Three more plain weave shots complete the basic design. Alternate gauze may also be woven with a 4/4 leno, followed by plain weave under four warp threads.

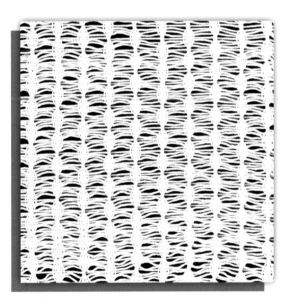

Alternate gauze.

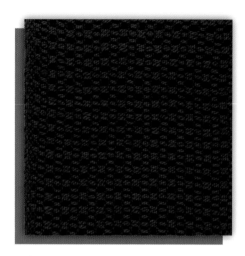

Left and right gauze.

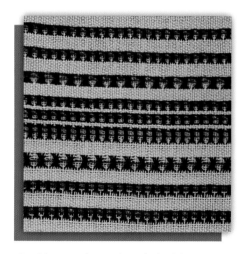

Double weave leno. 1/1 and 3/3 pick-up.

Left and Right Gauze

The Scottish cellular and thermo blankets were typically woven in left and right gauze with wool. The holes are evenly spaced, showing more texture and depth.

The weave is basically a 1/1 leno woven on a basket weave threading with each leno twisted opposite the previous twist. Thread the loom with yarns one and two in their own heddle on shaft one. Follow with the next two yarns in heddles on shaft two. Tie up treadle 1 to shaft 1 and treadle 2 on shaft 2. To weave, press the treadle 2 raising shaft two. While holding the upper threads right, reach to the lower shed to select the next thread. Bring it up and between the first and second thread pair on the upper shed and onto the pick-up stick. Let the upper threads drop under the pick-up stick. The next lower thread is brought up between the following top thread pair. When the pattern row is complete press treadle 1. Return the shuttle right with plain basket weave. Follow with two more basket weave shots and repeat.

Double Weave Leno

Double weave leno has two layers of two different colors, setting off the leno lace effects. The colors of each layer change from showing on the face to appearing in the background. The exchange of yarns from back to front interlocks the threads of the two layers. This keeps the tension of the two layers even, thus producing good selvages.

Select two contrasting-color yarns of the same size. Plan the warp thread count to be evenly divided by 12. The sett, or density, is closer than that of plain weave. A sett of 24 epi is good for 5/2 cotton. Wind the warp with both color yarns simultaneously. Thread the loom with the standard 4-shaft threading and tie-up. Thread the background yarns on shafts 1 and 3, with the face yarns of a lighter color on shafts 2 and 4. It is easier to weave with direct tie-up, with each treadle tied to a single shaft. Fill two shuttles, one for each color.

To weave plain-weave bands of light color on the top, follow these instructions: Press treadle 4, weave with light yarn, followed by treadle 2 with the light yarn. For the background layer, press treadles 2-3-4 to weave with the dark yarn, followed by pressing treadles 1-2-4 with dark yarn.

Weaving a leno lace band with the dark yarn on top, follow this pattern: Weave plain weave background by pressing treadle 1-3-4 using the light yarn, followed by treadles 1-2-3 and light yarn. Next form the leno pattern of your choice, pressing treadles 1-3 using dark yarn. Treadle 3 is the dark yarn plain weave return. Follow with plain-weave background by pressing treadles 1-3-4 using light yarn, then 1-2-3 with light yarn.

Finnish Lace

This is a fine airy leno background with a plain-weave motif or border. Sometimes an accent of a larger leno is incorporated in the design. Linen works especially well for this leno.

If 16/2 linen is used, the best sett is 20 epi. The total warp ends must be evenly divisible by eight if the design is centered on two twists. Before beginning, chart the design onto graph paper. Threading and tie-up is for plain weave. This is one of just a few lenos that require the first shed to have the right warp thread down. Begin by weaving a few rows of plain weave to spread the warp, with the shuttle starting at the right selvage.

Weave a row or two consisting of only background leno. Press treadle 2 and pick up 2/2 leno. This is done by pulling the upper two threads right while picking up the next two lower threads onto the pick-up stick. Let the two threads from the upper shed fall under the pick-up stick. Following the leno row, press treadle 1 to weave the tabby return right. This completes the pattern.

Now weave the beginning of the motif. Prepare small shuttles with yarn for each motif. The yarn may be the same yarn as the background or use an accent color. A slightly heavier yarn also works well. Note that there are two shots in the motif for every shot of background. With the background thread, pick up 2/2 leno onto the pick-up stick as before until the motif is reached. Let the pick-up stick go through the open shed in the motif area. Continue on with 2/2 leno background. Follow with a firm beat. On the same shed, lay in the pattern thread at the motif from left to right. Change the shed and lay in the motif thread right to left. Return the background shuttle right in tabby as before. Follow with two more rows in the motif areas, as before. Experiment with different yarns and setts. Incorporate 4/4 leno within the motif if desired, to enhance the design.

Norwegian Leno

If a very lacy effect is desired, Norwegian leno is the best choice. There is a distinctive "X" effect in the design between the rows. The design is achieved in a three-row sequence.

Use the standard threading and tie-up. With treadle 1 pressed, pick up 2/2 leno, working from right to left. Return the shuttle with tabby. The second pattern row has a combination of pick up leno. Begin with 1/2 leno, pick up one and drop two, twice. Pick up the first thread from the bottom shed and onto the pick-up stick. Let the two threads from the upper shed drop under the pick-up stick. Pick up 1/1 leno across the warp until six threads remain. End the row with 2/1 leno twice, pick up two and drop one. Press treadle 2 and tabby back, repeat. Note that when picking up the thread in 1/1 leno, the picked up thread lies under the left upper threads.

Finnish lace.

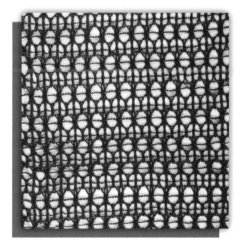

Norwegian leno.

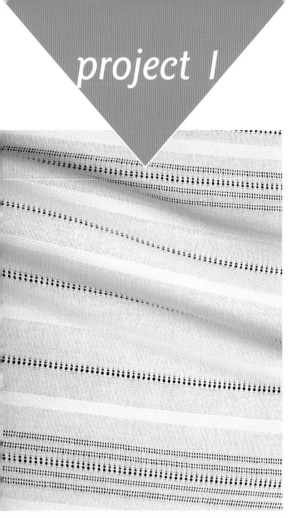

project 1

Mixed Pick Up Leno Runner

Design: Mixed pick up leno
Purpose: Runner
Warp: 8/2 mercerized cotton, 3,360 ypp
Weft: 8/2 mercerized cotton, 3,360 ypp
Sett: 18 epi
Reed: 18 dent
PPI: 18
Threading and Treadling: As for plain weave
Warp Ends: 272 ends
Warp Length: 2 yards (includes hems and loom waste)
Width at Reed: 15"
Finished Width: 13.25"

WEAVING: Weave leno patterns at will or follow guide below.

   1. Weave 2" plain weave.

   2. Weave one pattern row of 1/1 leno following directions above.

   3. Weave bands of plain weave and twill.

   4. Weave 1/1 or 2/2 leno.

   5. Weave bands of plain weave and bands of twill.

   6. Weave 2/2 leno.

   7. Weave a band of plain weave.

   8. Reverse the design sequence to complete the runner.

FINISHING: See "Finishing Cloth" on page 31. Turn hems up to the first leno row and stitch by hand.

project 2

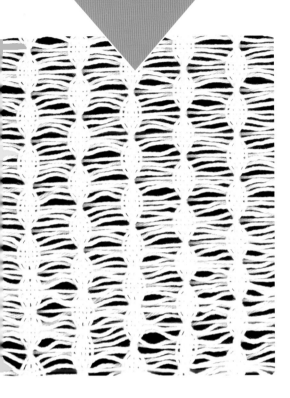

Alternate Gauze Curtains

Design: Alternate Gauze
Purpose: Curtains
Warp: 10/2 mercerized cotton, 4,200 ypp
Weft: 10/2 mercerized cotton, 4,200 ypp
Sett: 28 epi
Reed: 14 dent
PPI: 24–28
Threading and Treadling: As for plain weave
Warp Ends: 840 ends
Warp Length: Enough for curtains plus hems
Width at Reed: 30"
Finished Width: 28"

WEAVING:

1. Begin at right selvage using a closed shed.

2. Pull threads 1-2-3 left. Pull threads 4-5-6 right and onto pick-up stick.

3. Press treadle 1 raising the right selvage thread and pass pick-up stick through the shed under the first three threads. Close the shed and pick up 3/3 leno, as before.

4. Continue across warp in the same manner.

5. Press treadle 2 and tabby back.

6. Follow with two more rows of plain weave, three in all.

7. Begin the next pattern row, sliding the pick-up stick under three threads as for plain weave, followed by another 3/3 leno, offsetting the leno from the previous pattern row.

8. Follow with three shots of plain weave and repeat.

FINISHING: See "Finishing Cloth" on page 31. Turn and sew hems.

Plain bead leno using
novelty yarn. *Courtesy of
Unique Images.*

3. BEAD LENO

Bead leno is a loom-controlled leno. It is magical, mysterious, and possible.

You will discover a new joy as you expand your repertoire

of weaving techniques.

In this technique, warp ends lying parallel to each other twist together when the treadle is pressed—automatically! The warp ends actually move out of their usual position and cross over adjacent warp threads and are locked in place by the weft. The "bead" is the mechanical means that works together with the loom to create leno patterns. Textures and patterns range from plain gauze to blocks, stripes, and even decorative designs. The bead never appears in the finished cloth.

The next chapter expands on the many varieties of patterns. For now, we will dig deep into the basics, the tricks, and the secrets of weaving bead leno.

When examining leno textiles to determine the method by which they were created, start by looking at the interlacement of the threads. Bead leno textiles are recognized by the basket-weave seen in the untwisted portions. You will also notice that within one sample, all the leno twists have the same number of threads in the twist, lengthwise. True plain weave is noticeably absent.

⚬ Advantages of Bead Leno ⚬

A truly beautiful lace cloth can be woven that is lightweight yet possesses enough strength to be durable. Pressing a treadle then throwing the shuttle to create the twist can be seen as a shortcut for weaving leno. It is more accurate than picking up every twist onto the pick-up stick across the width of the warp, individually, by hand. With three to four picks per inch, it weaves up very quickly. The advantages of bead leno outweigh even doup leno, another type of loom-controlled leno. The doup method requires the creation of half heddles, which are then tied to the shafts.

⚬ Disadvantages of Bead Leno ⚬

Although there is the extra step of threading beads onto the warp, it goes fairly quickly. Once the warp is beaded you are limited to twists and basket weave. Plain weave is not possible with bead leno. One of the challenges of weaving bead leno is the restricted shed, sometimes called a forced shed. You will want to carefully follow all the steps to weaving successful bead leno to overcome this disadvantage.

⚬ Tools for Weaving Successful Bead Leno ⚬

Beads

The bead is the most important tool for weaving trouble-free bead leno. Many types of beads have been tested in the past with less than perfect results. Do not use cut sections of drinking straws, as they are abrasive to the thread and collapse during weaving. The ideal bead has a smooth, large hole, and its overall size is small enough to keep it from catching the neighboring bead. The bead I have found to work best is the "pony bead," or "mini pony bead." Pony beads are easy to find in stores and are inexpensive. They work well for medium to coarse threads and will not pass through the reed. For fine silk, a smaller bead is needed because of the denser sett and use of a finer reed. A small "jump ring" works well in this case. The ring is available as a jewelry finding.

The Loom

A 4-shaft loom is the basic loom required to weave bead leno. It may be a jack or countermarch, table or floor loom. It is also possible to weave bead leno on a rigid heddle loom. A deeper shed loom, which has a greater distance between the breast beam and the beater, is ideal for problem-free weaving. More shafts are required when more variety in design is desired. A simple leno or lengthwise stripe can be woven on an 8-shaft loom. Plan four more shafts for each additional block or step in the design. A second beam is required when weaving warp stripes combined with basket weave. The twists draw up much more warp than the basket weave portion of the pattern, causing tension problems unless a loom with two back beams is used.

Pick-Up Stick

The pick-up stick is required for achieving a clear shed. Slipping it into the shed helps you visually verify that the threads are picked up correctly and thus lift the shed for the shuttle. The stick needs to be 1.5" wide. The length should be at least as long as the width of the warp. A 20" pick-up stick works well for an 18" wide warp.

Temple

A temple is required to prevent draw-in or loss in width. The temple counteracts the natural draw-in from the twisting warp threads. It also helps maintain good tension throughout the warp. The temple should be as long as the width of the warp measured at the reed.

Shuttle

Most shuttles can be used for bead leno. With limited shed space, the height of the shuttle is important and must not exceed 1.25". A two-bobbin shuttle is nice when a doubled weft is used. When using a boat or end-delivery shuttle, do not overfill the bobbin, since an overfilled bobbin may catch on the warp.

↶ Fiber Selections ↷

Select the yarn carefully. Will the piece you plan be light and airy, or dense enough for clothing? The fiber you use must lend itself to the look of the textile you desire, as well as work successfully with this technique. If the yarn breaks easily, it is not a candidate for warp. Tug on the yarn to test the strength. Sticky or fuzzy yarns also are not good warp candidates because they cause the beads to stick together. They also restrict shifting of threads in the reed. Contrary to conventional wisdom, the warp yarn does not need to have a lot of give. Mercerized cotton is the best warp choice. It is smooth and strong. Linen also works well—even though it has no stretch or give. Wool has too much give and is fuzzy enough to get caught in the beads and reed. It is best to save this yarn for weft. Finely sett silk or rayon is very beautiful for bead leno, however, avoid using silk noil or other "slub" yarns for the warp as they may catch on the bead.

Often, a combination of fibers, one for the warp, and one for the weft, works well. Contrary to popular belief, a fine warp works well when combined with heavier weft. For other yarns, you can balance four-thread leno twists with a doubled weft yarn or yarn twice the size of the warp yarn. You could use 10/2 cotton warp and 5/2 or 8/2 cotton weft. If a lacy effect is not the focal point, try a novelty yarn or handspun for the weft. The strength of the warp twists stabilizes a sleazy weft. For a very lacy effect, use the finer threads widely sett. Explore specialty materials such as wire and plastics. The possibilities are only limited by availability.

↶ Color Effects ↷

There are several things to consider when selecting colors. One of the characteristics of bead leno is that the warp threads are the dominant thread. The warp threads show twice as much as the weft. Try weaving a color gamp with 1" sections of each color, closely sett. Use a weft the same colors as the warp, rotating through the colors in the same manner. You will see that the resulting cloth shows only warp stripes of color. It is best to do your color designing in the warp.

Another unique characteristic of bead leno is that it is possible to have a different color showing on each side of the cloth. To accomplish this, two threads of one color are threaded through the bead; the other color threads are not beaded. To add more depth to the color, use a weft color that is darker yet close in value to the warp yarn.

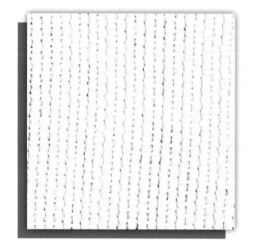

Fine silk warp with heavy wool weft.

Color gamp using 10/2 cotton.
Colors are warp dominant.

⤮ **Threading Rules for Bead Leno** ⤮

Threading the Shafts

The best threading to use for bead leno is a straight draw—1-2-3-4 (see Figure 3-1). The threads on shafts 1 and 4 are threaded onto the bead. Alternatively, you have the same effect if you thread 2-3-4-1 (see Figure 3-2). In this case, the threads on shafts 1 and 2 are threaded onto the bead. Since the threads that are not on the bead are stationary, they could be threaded on the same shaft, for example 1-2-2-3 as seen in Figure 3-3. Freeing up some shafts allows for a five-block design on a 16-shaft loom. It is not recommended to thread both threads on shaft 2 through the same heddle. Three-thread leno—threaded 1-2-3—is another possibility. The threads on shafts 1 and 3 are beaded; the thread on shaft 2 is the stationary thread. This is possible, but not recommended. The downside of this threading is that the twists do not look balanced. The unbalanced basket weave is not as pleasing to the eye either.

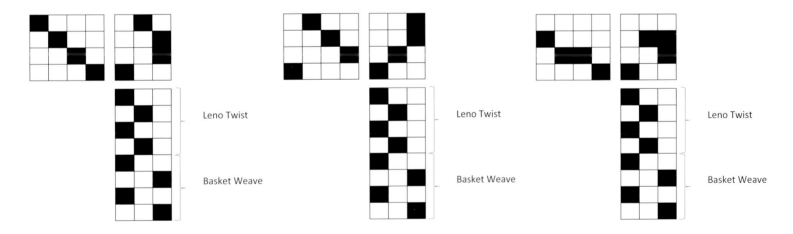

Figure 3-1. Threading draft for 4-shaft bead leno. Figure 3-2. Alternate threading draft for bead leno. Figure 3-3. Alternate threading draft for bead leno.

Sett

Think about the spacing of the warp. What will the finished cloth be used for? If you set the warp too close, the beads tend to catch on each other. However, if you want fewer spaces between the threads for clothing, it may be worth the effort. If your warp is spaced far apart, you will achieve a lacier effect. Remember you have four threads to every twist or unit, making your fabric seem like a heavier cloth than it is. The chart below helps you compare plain weave sett to bead leno sett. The three samples in the photograph show the effects of three different setts on the cloth produced. Every sample has a good sett. The sample on the left is a suitable weight for a scarf, while the one on the right is best used for a light jacket. Sample, to discover what works best for your project.

SETT COMPARISON PLAIN WEAVE TO BEAD LENO

Yarn	Plain Weave epi	Bead Leno epi
20/2	24 – 30	48 – 56
10/2	24 – 28	32 – 48
5/2	15 – 18	20 – 32

Sett study in 20/2 cotton. Left to right, sett 40 epi, 48 epi, 56 epi.

Design

The bead leno sett uses far more threads per inch than plain weave due to the four-thread twists. On graph paper, design the spaces and placement of the twists. How many twists per inch look best for the weight of the warp yarn? Determine if four threads will easily fit into a dent in the reed. Use a reed size no finer than 10 dpi for fine silk, or 6 to 8 dpi for 10/2 cotton. You also may skip dents to achieve your design. For example, the photograph shows the fabric that results when dents are skipped in an irregular pattern. The spacing in this example is varied. Some spaces are two dents; others are only a single dent. The information contained in the chart below is helpful when you create a pattern of this type. Using this warp calculations chart, find the dents needed for your pattern. The warp width is needed when threading the reed. Next count the number of dents in your pattern that are threaded in each repeat. By calculating the total ends needed, you can then measure out your warp. To help in evenly spreading the warp threads in a raddle, refer to the chart to determine ends per inch. Verify that the total number of ends is evenly divisible by four (eight when twisting fringe).

Lacy leno with irregular warp spacing.

WARP CALCULATIONS:

Total Dents Needed = Dents in Pattern × Pattern Repeat + Dents in Pattern to Balance

Warp Width (used for centering) = Dents Needed / Reed Size

Total Ends = Dents Threaded in Pattern × Pattern Repeat + Pattern Threads to Balance × 4

Ends Per Inch (to spread warp in raddle) = Total Ends / Warp Width

Threading Bead Leno

Measure the warp following your design and using the warp calculations chart then beam it smoothly onto your loom. Bead leno is one technique that requires beaming and threading the loom from the back to the front. Once beamed, thread the heddles following your chosen threading sequence. Next grab the first four threads coming from the heddles. Separate out the center two threads and lay them out of the way on top of the shaft. Thread a bead onto the outer two threads (see Figure 3-4). Join all four threads together and tie a slip knot to keep the bead in place. Continue in this manner across the warp. It is best to not leave the lease sticks in the warp, as it restricts the shed size.

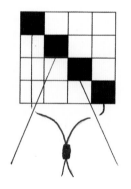

Figure 3-4. Proper placement of the bead on warp threads.

Beaded threads on loom, ready for weaving.

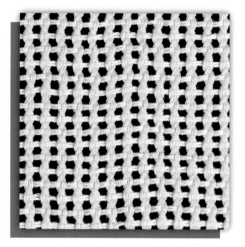

Bead leno warp thread twists left then right.

Begin sleying the reed, following the spacing in your pattern. It is very important that all four threads in the unit are threaded through one dent in the reed. Do not split a leno unit into a neighboring dent. Tie the warp threads onto the apron rod and set a firm tension. **Note that the beads on the warp are in front of the heddles and behind the reed.** The photograph shows a properly threaded warp. Refer to one of the threading diagrams to tie up the treadles (Figure 3-1, 3-2, or 3-3).

Treadling

Weaving the twist requires treadling one of the threads in the bead then the other. With the standard threading, treadle shaft 1 then shaft 4, repeatedly for all leno twists. The twist turns first to the left, as in all lenos. On the next shot, the twist returns to the right. In the photo, observe the left and right twisting of the warp. When basket weave is desired, treadle shaft 1 then shaft 2 and 3 together.

⤳ Weaving Successful Bead Leno ⤳

Now you are ready to weave. When using the same yarn for the weft as used for the warp, fill the bobbins of two shuttles or the two bobbins in a double-bobbin shuttle. The weft yarn needs to be double the size of the warp to achieve balanced twists and balanced basket weave. Weave a basket-weave header to spread the warp. Set the temple. Lay the temple upside down at the reed to gauge the correct length. Turn the temple over and place it on the warp, digging the teeth into the edges of the warp. Move it often.

When treadling the twist, extra care is required to clear the shed. You can free any tangled beads by pressing the basket weave treadle but not throwing a shuttle. You may find just reaching behind the reed and strumming your fingers across the beads while pressing the treadle will free up any tangled beads.

Next insert the pick-up stick through the shed. Turn the stick up on edge. Examine the threads, making sure you see only pairs of threads. When you are sure of your shed, send the shuttle through the shed right next to the pick-up stick. Remove the pick-up stick. Beat firmly. Follow the chart below.

WEAVING PROCESS

1. Set a tight warp tension.
2. Adjust and set temple.
3. Press the treadle for twist.
4. Strum beads to untangle.
5. Slip the pick-up stick into the shed, tip stick on edge.
6. Examine the warp patterning along the edge of the pick-up stick. The threads must lie in pairs. If not, press another treadle, not throwing a shuttle, and go back to #4 to begin again.
7. With the pick-up stick tipped on edge, push it forward then send the shuttle through in front of the pick-up stick.
8. Remove the pick-up stick. Beat firmly.
9. Advance the warp often.

Take-up and Draw-in

In bead leno, the take-up or loss in warp length can be fairly significant. The loss of warp length during weaving is due to the twisting of the warp threads. On average, the take-up is about 14%. For looser setts, it is best to add an additional 25% in warp length. The width draws in about 8% to 10% when using a temple.

FINISHING CLOTH

1. Hem stitch ends on the loom.
2. Wash in warm soapy water, soaking 10 minutes then agitating 2 minutes.
3. Rinse well.
4. Lay flat on towel to dry.
5. Lightly press, while barely damp, with press cloth.

project 1

Plain Bead Leno Scarf

Design: Plain Bead Leno
Purpose: Scarf
Warp: 10/2 mercerized cotton (4,200 ypp)
Weft: 8/2 Tencel (3,360 ypp)
Sett: 32 epi
Reed: 8 Dent
PPI: 6
Threading and Treadling: See Figure 3-1
Warp Ends: 320
Warp Length: 3 yd
Width at Reed: 10"
Finished Width: 9"

FINISHING: See "Finishing Cloth" on page 31.

Project 1. Scarf with magenta
warp and royal blue weft.
Courtesy of Eric Rice Photography.

project 2

Weft Stripe Bead Leno Yardage

Design: Weft Stripe
Purpose: Yardage for sweater or jacket
Warp: 2/8 Orlon (3,360 ypp)
Weft: 2/8 Orlon (3,360 ypp), doubled
Sett: 40 epi
Reed: 10 Dent
PPI: 8
Threading and Treadling: See Figure 3-1
Warp Ends: 720
Warp Length: Enough for project
Width at Reed: 18"
Finished Width: 17"

WEAVING: Weave 5 shots basket weave, then 3 shots leno twist. Repeat.

FINISHING: See "Finishing Cloth" on page 31.

Project 2. Yardage with horizontal stripes.

Tailored jacket,
block bead leno.
Courtesy of Unique Images.

4. PATTERN TECHNIQUES IN BEAD LENO

Advanced pattern techniques in bead leno open up new possibilities as you create one-of-a-kind textiles. Whether you are weaving table linens, scarves, or even clothing, you will be rewarded with all you create.

In bead leno, there are only two leno stitch choices. There are twists and there are non-twists of basket weave; that's it. Combining the twists and basket weave can be very creative and result in some very beautiful textiles. This chapter shows you some of the possibilities that you can use in creating your own patterns. Really, the possibilities are endless.

☙ Bead Leno Blocks ☙

Blocks add interest to the overall cloth. Squares or rectangles of lace balanced with basket weave are quite versatile. Uses range from clothing to scarves. Try a scarf in a widely spaced warp using fine threads. In the photo on page 34 we see heavier cloth created with a fine, strong cotton warp, which locks the bulky wool weft in place as blocks are formed. The textile is stable enough to be tailored.

Leno blocks have all the characteristics of a unit weave. Block A is all leno twists while block B weaves basket weave. To weave two blocks, eight shafts are usually required. Once the sett is established the repeats for each block will be known. Thread the loom following the threading draft in Figure 4-1. For each of the four thread units, the threads on shaft 1 and 4 go through the bead and the threads on 5 and 8 are beaded. Treadle each block following your design. When weaving two squared blocks, the tension of leno versus basket weave is always balanced. However, be cautioned as you design other block patterns. Be sure to weave each block equally to avoid tension problems.

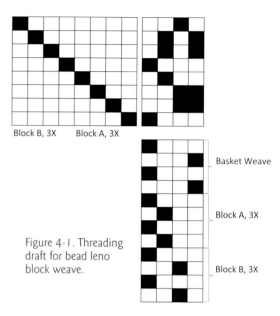

Block B, 3X   Block A, 3X

Basket Weave

Block A, 3X

Figure 4-1. Threading draft for bead leno block weave.

Block B, 3X

Four Shaft Blocks

The best way to design blocks is to space the threads out on eight shafts. There is another way to weave blocks using only a four shaft loom. Observe that while block A creates leno twists, block B creates the basket weave. In block A the threads on shaft 1 and 4 are beaded. For the threads in block B, 1 and 3 are on a bead. Follow the treadling on the threading draft in Figure 4-2. Although it is possible to weave a two-block leno on four shafts, it is more challenging. If there is a limitation of shafts, this may be worth the effort. The threads do not shift as easily, because the threads are closer together. There will be a double shed, so using the pick-up stick, carefully select the lowest shed. Follow all the tips for weaving bead leno presented in chapter 3.

Block B   Block A

Block A Leno, Block B Basket

Block A Basket, Block B Leno

Figure 4-2. Threading draft for 4-shaft block weave.

Vertical Stripes

Use your imagination when designing stripes. Leno stripes in a heavier thread than the basket weave stripe can be stunning. Another option is to outline the leno stripes with the outer four-thread unit in another color or thread weight. Stripes of leno twists and basket weave can be beautiful. Vertical stripes are threaded as a block weave, but treadled for one block only.

You will find one of the challenges to be the difference in take-up between the leno and basket weave stripes. The leno twists draw up more warp as you weave than the plain basket weave. If you plan to weave more than 15 inches in length, a second beam will be necessary. The threads for the basket weave go onto one beam. Measure 25% more warp for the leno stripes and place the warp threads on the second beam. Weaving stripes is best done on eight shafts. Follow the threading draft in Figure 4-1, threading the first four shafts for the planned width of that stripe. Then thread the other stripe on shafts 5 through 8. Follow just one of the treadling sequences on the threading draft. Then refer to chapter 3 for the weaving process.

Bead leno, vertical stripes.

Mirror Bead Leno

Mirror bead leno is named "mirror" because the threading for each of the four thread units are a mirror of the unit next to it. Threading in this manner creates a smocked appearance. This textile is useful for lacy scarves and fine wool for clothing, for example. Try a coarse thread widely spaced for the bodice of a garment. The #3 crochet cotton is the perfect weight for a sweater, as seen in the photo at right. Thread the loom by threading shafts 1-2-3-4 followed by threading shafts 4-3-2-1. Note that each threading unit must be a full set of four threads. All units have the threads on shafts one and four on a bead. One unit twists to the left while the next unit twists to the right. This design causes more draw-in than any other leno design due to the opposing twists. A temple will be necessary. To weave the sample in the photo, thread the loom with a sett of 16 epi. Weave using a single weft.

Mirror design bead leno.

∽ Mixed Bead Leno Patterns ∽

What if leno twists were combined with basket weave and mirror leno? This vest is designed with the darker stripes threaded in mirror leno, while the lighter stripes are basket weave. A heavier variegated thread sets off the stripes. It is best to put the threads for the basket weave on one beam with the leno twist threads on the second beam. If a second beam is not available, plan to weave about fifteen inches before removing it from the loom, weaving enough for one pattern piece at a time if weaving for clothing and re-tying between each piece.

Using the same principle as above, the design can be combined in a way to show diagonal patterns within the cloth, as seen in the photo. Weave with a doubled weft when using a finer yarn. When weaving a mixed design such as this, the challenge is getting a clear shed. Carefully select the lowest shed with a pick-up stick. Follow the weaving tips in chapter 3.

Vest woven in mixed bead leno using 10/2 cotton. *Courtesy of Unique Images*.

Mixed bead leno, using 10/2 cotton. *Courtesy of Unique Images*.

Bead Leno Double Weave

Bead leno in double weave is fun and easy. It is best used for items like wall hangings or table runners. Weave with the basket weave on the background and leno twists on the top. At the selvages the layers are connected by interlocking the threads of the two shuttles at the edges. One thing to watch for is the draw-in of the upper leno layer. The background basket weave is not as tight. Pull the weft snugly when weaving the basket weave to balance the difference between the two layers. More shots of the basket weave may be required than that of the leno layer. Thread the loom in a straight draw. Follow the threading draft in Figure 4-3. All of the four thread units are beaded and in their own dent in the reed.

Bead leno double weave runner in 5/2 cotton, sett 40 epi.

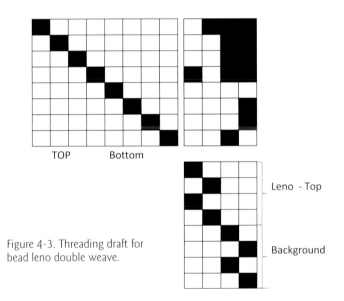

TOP   Bottom

Leno - Top

Background

Figure 4-3. Threading draft for bead leno double weave.

Mirror Bead Leno Sweater

Design: Mirror Bead Leno
Purpose: Yardage for a sweater
Warp: 2/8 Orlon (3,360 ypp)
Weft: 2/8 Orlon (3,360 ypp), doubled
Sett: 48 epi
Reed: 12 Dent
PPI: 6
Threading and Treadling: See Figure 4-4
Warp Width: 3 inches wider than pattern piece
Warp Length: Enough for project

FINISHING: See "Finishing Cloth" on page 31.

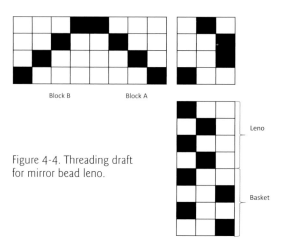

Figure 4-4. Threading draft
for mirror bead leno.

Project 1. Mirror bead leno with fine Orlon.

project 2

Mixed Design Bead Leno Vest

Design: Mixed design
Purpose: Vest yardage
Warp: 10/2 mercerized cotton (4,200 ypp)
Weft: 10/2 mercerized cotton (4,200 ypp), doubled
Sett: 36 epi
Reed: 10 Dent
PPI: 9
Threading and Treadling: See Figure 4-5.
Warp Width: 3 inches wider than pattern piece
Warp Length: Enough for project

NOTE: Two beams are best, or weave 15" then cut off and re-tie

FINISHING: See "Finishing Cloth" on page 31.

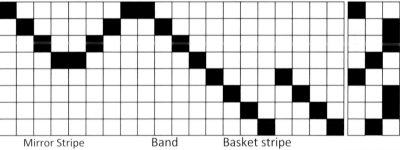

Mirror Stripe Band Basket stripe

Figure 4-5. Threading draft for
mixed design bead leno.

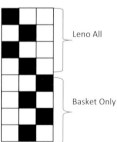

Leno All

Basket Only

Project 2. Vest woven in mixed bead leno.
Courtesy of Unique Images.

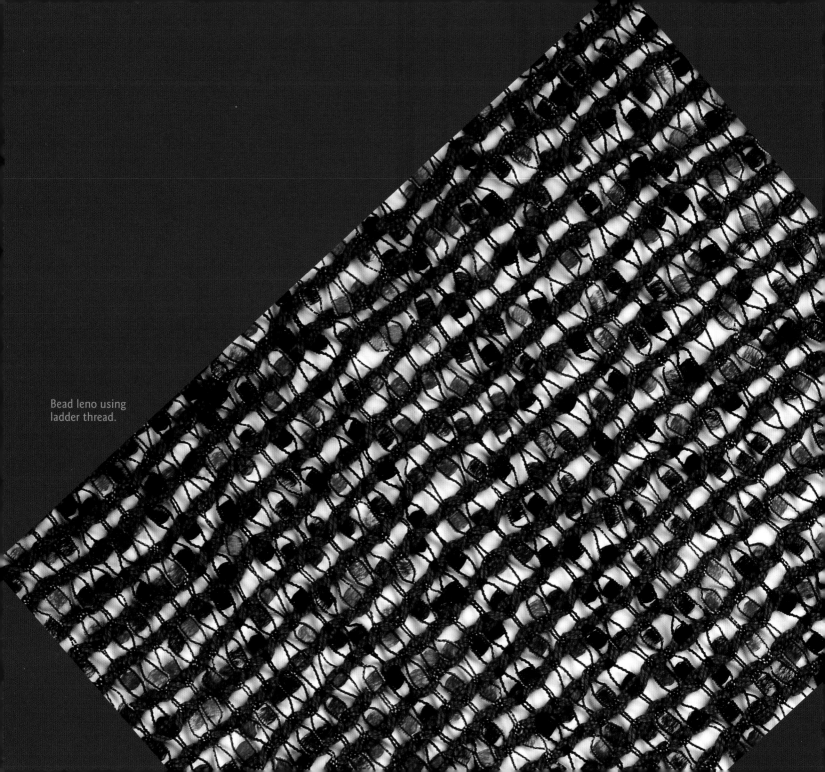

Bead leno using
ladder thread.

5. PUSHING THE LIMITS OF BEAD LENO

How far can we push the limits of bead leno? We traditionally see leno used for the light and lacy textile it produces. It doesn't have to be just for that. Designing new ideas in bead leno can be inspired by personal favorites or one's own life experiences.

The colors we choose to weave with certainly come about that way. What if bead leno was used for clothing? Could the structure withstand a curved neckline, or arm hole? A loosely sett leno would not work. In fact, the warp threads would slide out of place and become distorted. But if leno is sett closer or if we use yarns that grip each other, it would be structurally sound.

Let's explore ways to create and finish cloth in bead leno that is out of the ordinary.

Bead leno woven in thick and thin wool with 20/2 silk warp.

Bead leno with novelty wool yarn.

Novelty Yarns

Many weavers in the past suggested using only certain yarns for leno. But, thinking more creatively, what about ladder thread, such as Plymouth Yarn® Eros Drifters? In the photo on page 42, ladder thread is used for weft. The grist of the thread keeps the structure stable, yet the cloth is lacy and suitable for clothing.

Other novelty weft yarns such as thick and thin offer even greater variety; see the photo at left. A great textural look is created using bulky thick-and-thin wool for the weft. The space-dyed looped wool in the photo below has a fine, smooth wool warp, making the cloth suitable for a sweater. When using novelty yarns a single weft is used. The leno locks the weft in place and shows the unique quality of the yarn.

There is no limit to the yarns we can use for leno. Weave a sample to see what meets your needs. Novelty threads add a creative accent to any piece. In the photo at right, a yarn called Fun Fur from Lion Brand Yarn® is used in the borders for the shawl. Can you envision Fun Fur used in a sweater?

Elastic thread has many more uses than the ones for which it was originally invented. The conventional use of elastic thread is to attain a shirred effect when sewing clothing. In the photo at far right, we see an example of elastic thread used at the wrist of a dress. Just slip the spool of elastic thread onto a boat shuttle for weaving. Using basket weave treadling, insert the shuttle and pull the elastic 50% before beating in place. A temple is required to maintain the width of the warp. Wouldn't this work well for the bodice of a sundress?

Bead leno shawl
with Fun Fur accent.
Courtesy of Eric Rice Photography.

Dress sleeve with
elastic thread weft.
Courtesy of Unique Images.

✁ Bead Leno in Other Structures ✁

Bead leno can be incorporated into other weaving structures to add strength to the cloth, or used to resemble tucking on a bodice. In the photo at right a single bead leno twist is incorporated into the huck lace design, another weave structure. The cloth is woven using Jagger Spun Zephyr® warp and weft and sett at 26 epi. The leno is threaded on shafts 5 through 8, while the huck lace pattern is on shafts 1 through 4. The leno threads need to be on a second beam because they draw up more thread in the twists. See Figure 5-1 for the threading draft. Experiment with the possibilities.

Huck lace technique with bead leno accent.

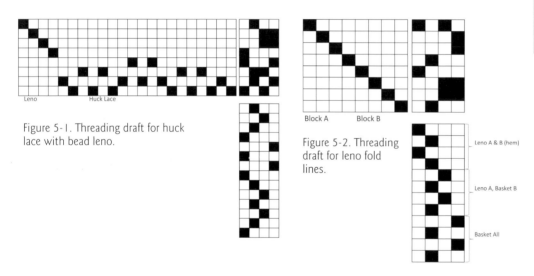

Figure 5-1. Threading draft for huck lace with bead leno.

Figure 5-2. Threading draft for leno fold lines.

✁ Clothing Finishes ✁

The structure of leno compared to basket weave is more open. Taking advantage of that, a line of leno within a cloth of basket weave gives a line on which to fold. A sharp crease for a facing or hem is sometimes required when weaving with heavier threads such as wool or heavy cotton. In the photo at right we see a sample showing the facing and a hem folded on a line of leno. Think of this application for a jacket facing edge or even a hem for placemats. Follow the threading draft in Figure 5-2 to weave leno fold lines.

Bead leno used as fold line, at right and as a bottom hem.

Cutting Leno

Leno threads have a natural tendency to spring apart and fray when cut. One way to minimize this is to use iron-on interfacing. Depending on the hand of the finished cloth and the intended use for it, a lightweight knit interfacing will stabilize the cloth. The interfacing must have stretch. One that works well is a tricot knit interfacing such as Easy Knit® from Pellon®. Another is Fusi-Knit® (HTC Inc.).

Following manufacturer's instructions, use a damp press cloth and press with an iron set to medium heat. Interface the entire yardage. Lay out the pattern and cut. Take each piece directly to the serger to finish the cut edges.

Another method of cutting leno cloth is to use a 0.5" or 0.75" fusible tape. One type is sold under the name of Extremely Fine Knit Stay® from SewKeys E®. Fusing the tape at the cutting line provides a safe way to keep the threads from fraying. It is especially useful for lightweight cloth where interfacing would be too stiff.

Cutting bead leno.

FUSIBLE TAPE METHOD

1. Lay pattern pieces out on the wrong side of the cloth.

2. Place fusible tape along the cutting line. Using the pattern edges as a guide, extend the tape over the intended cut edge but not beyond the stitching line.

3. Fuse tape in place using a narrow iron (commonly used for quilting) set to medium heat.

4. Cut through the tape on the cutting line.

5. Take each piece directly to the serger to finish the edges.

Cut cloth using fusible tape.

French seam.

French Seam

On leno, seams need a good finished edge to encase the raw edges and keep from raveling. This is important even if the garment is lined. Serging works well for lined garments. For a lacy unlined leno garment consider a French seam.

FRENCH SEAM METHOD

1. Place the wrong sides of the cloth together along the seam line.

2. Stitch a 0.25" seam, using the side of the presser foot as a guide.

3. Refold the seam to the inside with the cloth now right sides together, encasing the raw edge. Baste, then press.

4. Machine stitch the seam 0.375" from the fold.

5. Lay the piece open with the wrong side up. Lay the seam to one side and press.

Hong Kong Seam

For an unlined garment the Hong Kong, or bound, seam provides a finish that can be decorative as well as functional.

HONG KONG SEAM METHOD

1. Cut strips of silk charmeuse or rayon lining fabric 1.75" wide, on the bias.

2. Tug a section of bias slightly to determine the right side. The strip will curl to fit the seam edge.

3. Lay the right side of the bias strip against the right side of the fabric, aligning the edge with the cut edge of the seam.

4. Sew 0.25" from the cut edge, using the edge of the presser foot as a guide.

5. Turn the bias strip encasing the cut edge to the underside and baste, then press.

6. Stitch in the ditch of the seam just created, to catch the underside of the bias. "Stitching in the ditch" is stitching from the right side exactly on top of the seam line.

Hong Kong seam.

Hems

Hems are just as important as seam finishes. They are sometimes seen when the garment is unlined, so it is important to take as much pride in finishing a garment as it was to weave the cloth. When the garment is lined, a serged edge is acceptable. Use a catch stitch as seen in Figure 5-3, to hand sew the hem before it is lined.

When the garment is unlined, a nice hem finish is the bound hem. The method is similar to the Hong Kong seam finish.

BOUND HEM METHOD

1. Follow steps 1 through 6 for Hong Kong seam.

2. Hand stitch hem using the catch stitch pictured in Figure 5-3.

Corded Edge

Leno cloth can sometimes be bulky. Creating a sharp edge on a jacket or vest front can seem impossible. A corded edge gives a professional-looking sharp edge. The lining will lay behind it nicely and not peek out.

CORDED EDGE METHOD

1. Cut bias strips of lining fabric or Ultrasuede® 1.5" wide.

2. Lay 0.125" polyester cording on the bias strip then fold the strip encasing the cording.

3. Machine stitch using a zipper foot, as close to the cording as possible.

4. Lay the cut edge of the finished cording against the seam edge of the garment. Clip as needed to fit corners.

5. Machine stitch the cording in place using a zipper foot and sewing on top of the previous stitching.

6. Lay the facing or lining against the garment with right sides together. Baste.

7. Machine stitch through all layers sewing on top of the stitching sewn in step 5.

8. Turn right side out and baste along the edge. Press.

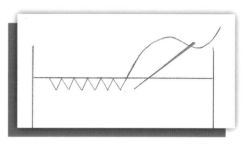

Figure 5-3. Hem finish using catch stitch.

Bound hem.

Corded edge.

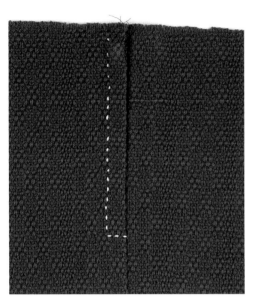

Zipper finish.

Zippers

We usually try not to use zippers in handwoven cloth because the cloth is unstable and stretchy. But sometimes we really need to. Follow these steps for a flawless zipper finish.

ZIPPER METHOD

1. When cutting out your garment, plan for a 1" seam allowance on the zipper seam.

2. Lightweight cloth may require fusible tape in the seam allowance to stabilize it.

3. Machine baste a 1" seam allowance for the zipper and press open.

4. Lay open a sheer zipper against the right side seam allowance with teeth butting against the basted seam line, following package instructions.

5. Machine baste the zipper to the seam allowance. Close the zipper. Turn the zipper so that the right side is face up.

6. Pull the seam back exposing the zipper teeth. Machine stitch close to the zipper using a zipper foot.

7. Lay the zipper back against the seam allowance and hand baste along the left side, through the zipper and garment.

8. Sew the final top-stitching by hand, with double thread. Use a pick stitch 0.375" from the seam line. A pick stitch is a very short backstitch on the outside, while the wrong side shows a longer stitch. See the photo for an example.

Bound Buttonholes

The most professional finish for handwoven garment is the bound buttonhole. It is nothing to be feared. There are several buttonhole methods used. The method that follows is my favorite. Follow these easy steps before attaching the facing.

Finished bound buttonholes.
Courtesy of Unique Images.

BOUND BUTTONHOLE METHOD

1. Determine the size of the buttonhole by measuring the width and the height of the button. Add these together to get the size of the buttonhole.

2. Stablize the buttonhole area by pressing a 2"-wide strip of fusible interfacing to the wrong side.

3. Mark the buttonholes on the outside of the garment. Run a basting stitch 0.5" from the front seam line, from the top of the garment to the bottom, as seen in the photo.

4. Sew another basting line parallel to the previous basting line. The distance from the other line is the size of the buttonhole, determined in step 1.

5. Mark the placement of each buttonhole with a thread, using a T-square.

6. Cut squares of binding for each buttonhole. The size of the square should be about 1.5" larger than the buttonhole.

7. Lay the binding square centered over each marked buttonhole, right side to right side. Use the basting lines as a guide for centering.

8. Machine stitch each side of the length of each buttonhole, 0.375" to 0.5" apart. Do not stitch the ends.

9. Cut the buttonhole open through the center, stopping 0.25" from the ends. Pivot and cut diagonally into the corners.

10. Pull the facing square to the inside, forming the welt. Baste in place.

11. Lift the ends to where the diagonal cuts can be seen. Stitch across.

12. From the right side, stitch in the ditch around the entire buttonhole to hold the welt in place. "Stitching in the ditch" is stitching from the right side exactly on top of the seam line.

13. After the facing is on the jacket, mark for cutting the back of the buttonhole. From the front, poke a straight pin through each end of the buttonhole from the right side. Cut the buttonhole open on the facing side, cutting in a straight line from pin to pin.

14. Tuck the raw edges of the facing in along the back of the buttonhole, forming an oval. Hand stitch in place.

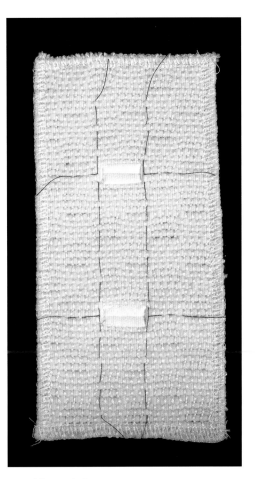

Bound buttonholes.

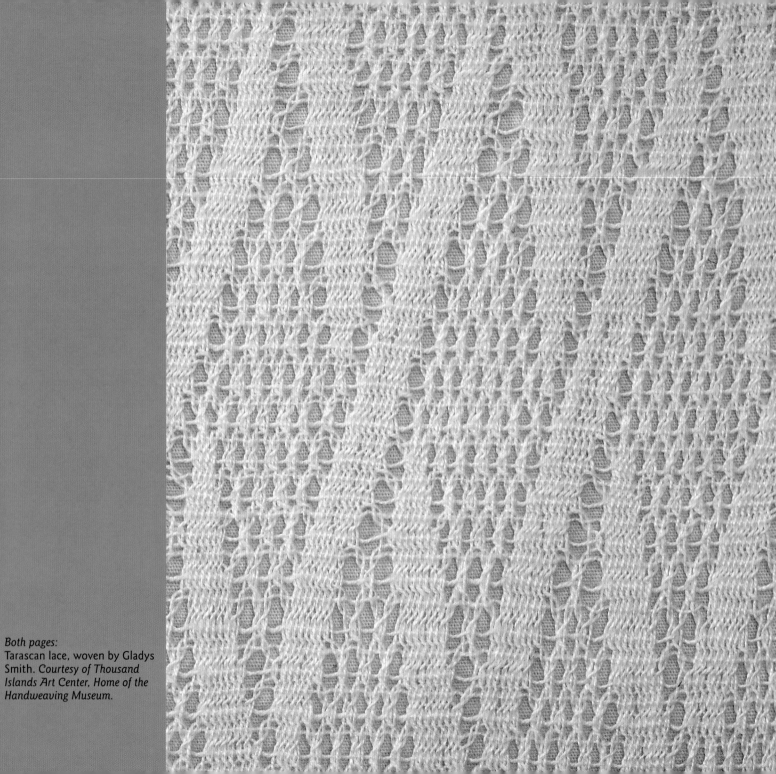

Both pages:
Tarascan lace, woven by Gladys
Smith. *Courtesy of Thousand
Islands Art Center, Home of the
Handweaving Museum.*

6. TARASCAN LACE

Tarascan lace is a hand-manipulated leno. Traditionally the Tarascan people wove their lace on a backstrap loom. Today we use the floor loom. Originally the Tarascos wove shawls of Tarascan lace. Today we use this technique for scarves and table coverings. Many times Tarascan lace is incorporated into clothing as an inset or motif.

   Though not Tarascan, Gladys Smith as well as Barbara Pascal specialized in this technique. Their linens were woven on a floor loom. The textiles were later donated by Richard Esparza to the Thousand Islands Art Center, Home of the Handweaving Museum, in Clayton, New York, in 2002. The photos seen here show some of the donated works. The traditional designs are recognized as Tarascan by their distinct diagonal lines and triangles. A true plain weave is possible within the cloth.

   The leno twist draws in at the selvages. This is most evident when spacing out bands of leno against bands of plain weave. To overcome the draw-in, use a temple and allow plenty of weft before beating. Tabby borders also help overcome draw-in.

Design

The design is basically a combination of hand-picked 1/1 leno for the pattern or motif and 2/2 leno for the background. Originally Tarascan lace was woven with fine overspun yarn of cotton or linen. For scarves and blouses of finer cloth use 20/2 cotton. Linen 40/2 works well for towels and mats, sett at 30 epi. Thread the loom as for plain weave (threaded 1-2-3-4). This threading makes it easy to select threads for each leno twist. The warp thread count must be evenly divisible by 4. Tarascan lace is woven on an open shed.

The native Tarascan weaver can visualize the pattern and does not write out a threading draft. We will use a written pattern. Lay out the pattern on graph paper that has 10 squares per inch. Each square represents one thread. Steep diagonal patterns of 1/1 leno are the typical pattern. The 1/1 pattern areas are always an odd number of twists within the project. To create the traditional design, every other pattern row is offset by starting and ending the row with one 1/1 leno. You will see that the 2/2 leno is split on the second pattern row, taking two threads from each of the previous two 2/2 leno twists. There must be a transition stitch between the background and the motif, using a three-thread leno. On the right side of the motif make a 2/1 leno and 1/2 leno on the left. The transition leno is written into the pattern at each side of the motif.

Basic Stitches

1/1 leno, sometimes called the pattern stitch, is a simple twisting of one thread around another thread. It is used to offset the pattern rows as well as for the design itself.

1. Press the treadle that raises the thread on shaft one. Begin at the right selvage.
2. With the left hand, pull the upper shed threads left.
3. With the pick-up stick or your fingers, pick up 1 thread from the lower shed and put it on the pick-up stick.
4. Let the next upper thread drop under the pick-up stick.
5. Work the designed pattern following your design.
6. Work the background leno to complete the row.
7. Following the pattern row, press the opposite treadle and return the shuttle to the right in plain weave.

2/2 leno consists of twisting 2 threads around 2. It is the background leno.

1. Work from the right with the treadle pressed that raises the thread on shaft one.
2. With the left hand, pull the upper shed threads left.
3. Pick up 2 threads from the lower shed and put them on the pick-up stick.
4. Let the next 2 upper threads drop under the pick-up stick.
5. Go to number 2 to complete the row.
6. Follow the row with a plain-weave return by pressing the opposite treadle.

2/1 or 1/2 leno is used as a transition stitch between the background and the motif. Three threads are twisted, 2/1 is on the right side of the motif and 1/2 is on the left side.

2/1 leno, right side of motif:

1. Pick up 2/2 background leno with treadle pressed, following your design pattern until the motif is reached.
2. Twist one transition stitch by pulling the upper shed threads left as you pick up 2 threads from the lower shed and put them on the pick-up stick.
3. Let 1 upper thread drop under the pick-up stick.
4. Continue following the design pattern with 1/1 leno for the motif or dominant pattern.

1/2 leno, left side of motif:

1. Pick up the 1/1 pattern until the left side of the motif is reached.
2. Create a transition stitch as before by pulling the upper shed threads left as you pick up 1 thread from the lower shed and put it on the pick-up stick.
3. Let 2 upper threads drop under the pick-up stick.
4. Continue following your pattern with 2/2 background leno to complete the row.

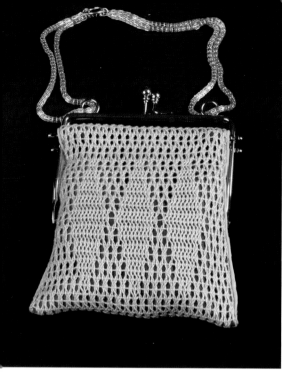

Tarascan lace purse. *Courtesy of Eric Rice Photography.*

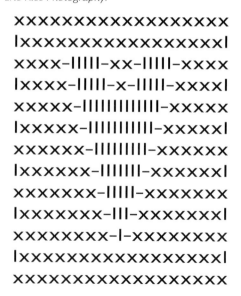

1. Weave with an open shed.

2. Thread the loom as for plain weave. Tie up treadles as for plain weave.

3. On every pattern row, the right selvage thread must be up when the treadle is pressed.

4. Use light tension.

5. Use a temple to prevent draw-in. Allow plenty of weft thread before beating.

6. Always work the pattern row right to left.

7. Always turn the pick-up stick on edge and check for errors. Push toward the reed.

8. Pass the shuttle to the left in front of the pick-up stick. Remove the pick-up stick and beat gently but firmly.

9. Every pattern row must be followed by a tabby row return.

Tabby Borders

Tabby borders are an optional part of Tarascan lace. It helps overcome the tendency to draw in for this type of leno. This technique is also called Spanish Lace.

The selvage border typically uses 12 threads on each side. There are three rows of plain weave in the border for every leno pattern row. With the shuttle at the right selvage and treadle pressed, weave plain weave for the first twelve threads, bringing the shuttle to the upper surface. Change the shed by pressing the opposite treadle. Return the shuttle right in plain weave. Change the shed and weave plain weave in the border then continue the leno pattern left as designed until twelve threads remain. Weave extra plain weave rows in the left border similar to the right. Be careful to maintain the same thread count throughout each border.

Figure 6-1. Project design key: "X" = 2/2 leno, "I" = 1/1 leno, "-" = 1/2 or 2/1 leno.

Tarascan Lace Sample

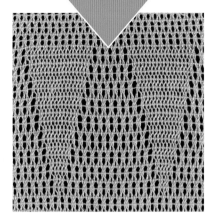

Design: Tarascan lace sample
Warp: 5/2 mercerized cotton (2,100 ypp)
Weft: 5/2 mercerized cotton (2,100 ypp)
Ends: 72
Sett: 16 epi
Reed: 8 Dent
Threading and Treadling: As for Plain Weave

WEAVING:

Weave a few shots of tabby to spread the warp. Follow the chart in Figure 6-1 from bottom to top, or the steps listed below. To prepare for weaving the pattern row, the shuttle must be at the right and have the first right selvage thread up when the treadle is pressed.

Project: Tarascan Lace Sample, double wide pattern.

1. Pick up 2/2 leno across all. Tabby back.

2. Pick up 1/1 once, 2/2 leno 17 times, 1/1 once. Tabby back.

3. Pick up 2/2 leno 8 times, 2/1 once, 1/1 leno once, 1/2 once, 2/2 leno 8 times. Tabby back.

4. Pick up 1/1 once, 2/2 leno 7 times, 2/1 once, 1/1 leno 3 times, 1/2 once, 2/2 leno 7 times, 1/1 once. Tabby back.

5. Pick up 2/2 leno 7 times, 2/1 once, 1/1 leno 5 times, 1/2 once, 2/2 leno 7 times. Tabby back.

6. Pick up 1/1 once, 2/2 leno 6 times, 2/1 once, 1/1 leno 7 times, 1/2 once, 2/2 leno 6 times, 1/1 once. Tabby back.

7. Pick up 2/2 leno 6 times, 2/1 once, 1/1 leno 9 times, 1/2 once, 2/2 leno 6 times. Tabby back.

8. Pick up 1/1 once, 2/2 leno 5 times, 2/1 once, 1/1 leno 11 times, 1/2 once, 2/2 leno 5 times, 1/1 once. Tabby back.

9. Pick up 2/2 leno 5 times, 2/1 once, 1/1 leno 13 times, 1/2 once, 2/2 leno 5 times. Tabby back.

10. Pick up 1/1 leno once, 2/2 leno 4 times, 2/1 once, 1/1 leno 5 times, 2/1 once, 2/2 once, 1/2 leno once, 1/1 leno 5 times, 1/2 once, 2/2 leno 4 times, 1/1 once. Tabby back.

11. Pick up 2/2 leno 4 times, 2/1 once, 1/1 leno 5 times, 2/1 once, 2/2 leno 2 times, 1/2 once, 1/1 leno 5 times,1/2 once, 2/2 leno 4 times. Tabby back.

12. Pick up 1/1 once, then 2/2 across, ending with one 1/1 once. Tabby back.

13. Pick up 2/2 leno across all. Tabby back.

FINISHING: See "Finishing Cloth" on page 31. Block using spray starch.

conclusion

We have discovered, throughout this book, that quite an array of leno weaves are possible. Three chapters here focused specifically on bead leno and its unique qualities. And taking into account the laciness of leno, we have learned to be especially prudent about sewing the leno textiles. You now know the "secrets" that lie within the leno weaves. As you have sampled them, you have broken the barrier of a problematic weave keeping so many of us from attempting the leno weaves.

Using the sparks of inspiration this book gives you for further exploration, follow your heart—and enjoy the newfound love for leno.

glossary

Cording – Heavy twisted threads appearing like rope, usually encased in cloth to use as a finished edge.

Dent – Space in the reed through which the warp is threaded.

Draft – A diagram of the threading order, tie-up, and treadling sequence.

Draw-in – Selvage pull-in when weaving.

Doup – A half heddle used as a tool to pull the warp thread to the side, causing a twist in the warp threads.

Dents Per Inch (dpi) – Measurement of dents in a reed.

End – An individual warp thread.

Ends Per Inch (epi) – The yarn or warp threads per inch.

Gamp – Cloth with sections of color or structure threaded equally, that are woven in the same intervals.

Gauze – All over leno cloth of twisted warp threads that are lightweight and sheer.

Heddle – Wire or cord with an eye, which is attached to the shaft.

Leno – A strong yet lacy cloth made up of warp thread that is twisted with the neighboring warp thread. It is sometimes combined with plain or basket weave.

Mercerized – Treated with a chemical process that gives sheen to cotton thread.

Mirror Leno – Consecutive leno units with opposing threading, causing a twist first left then right.

Raddle – A tool with pegs at regular intervals, used for spreading the warp during threading.

Pick – A single row of weft.

Pick-up Stick – Flat stick with a rounded point.

Picks Per Inch (ppi) – The measured density of the weft.

Selvage – The woven edge on either side of the cloth.

Sett – The density or spacing of threads in the warp.

Shaft – The frame that contains the heddles.

Shed – The opening or separation of the warp threads created by pressing a treadle for the shuttle to pass.

Shot – One throw of the shuttle.

Sley – Threading the reed.

Tabby – Plain weave in which the weft is interlaced with the warp threads.

Take-up – The loss of warp length that draws up as you weave.

Temple – An adjustable tool with teeth on either end, sometimes referred to as a stretcher. It is used to reduce draw-in and maintain the width of the cloth.

Threading Draft – The weaving pattern made up of the threading, tie-up, and treadling sequence.

Tie-up – Connection attaching shafts to the treadle on a floor loom.

Treadle – The pedal on the loom that, when pressed, raises the shafts.

Unit – A group of threads acting together.

Warp – The threads stretching from front to back on the loom.

Weft – The crosswise threads of the cloth.

Yards Per Pound (ypp) – Yarn size measurement.

bibliography

1. History

Anderson, Wayne. "Mexico's Tarasco Indians." 2010. http://www.berea.edu/foreignlanguages/studyabroad/spn-mltravel.

Alderman, Sharon. "Loom-Controlled Leno." *Handwoven*, May 1981.

Atwater, Mary. *American Handweaving*. New York: Macmillan, 1973.

———. "Peruvian Leno." *The Weaver*, March 1936.

———. "The Bead-Leno Weave." In *Practical Weaving Suggestions*, vol. XI. Shelby, NC: Lily Mills, 1950.

Becker, John. *Pattern and Loom*. Copenhagen: Rhodos Publishing, 1987.

Emery, Irene. *The Primary Structures of Fabrics*. Washington, DC: The Textile Museum, 1966.

Frey, Berta. "What Is Leno?" *Handweaver & Craftsman*, Spring 1955.

Gilroy, Clinton. *The Art of Weaving by Hand and Power*, New York: George D. Baldwin Publishers, 1844.

Graetzer, Margarita. "Morelia Mexico." 2011. http://www.berea.edu/foreignlanguages/studyabroad/spn-mltravel.

Murphy, John. *Treatise on the Art of Weaving*. Edinburgh, Scotland: Glasgow Blackie and Sons, 1845.

Schoeser, Mary. *World Textiles*. New York: Thames & Hudson, 2003.

Sullivan, Donna. "Gauze Weave." *Shuttle Spindle & Dyepot*, Summer 1986.

———. "Leno for Four." *Weaver's*, no. 15, 1991.

Tidball, Harriet. *The Handloom Weaves*. Shuttle Craft Guild Monograph 33. Freeland, WA: HTH Publishers, 1957.

Watson, William. *Advanced Textile Design*. New York: Longman's Green and Company, 1947.

Weaver, Joan K. *Spinning and Weaving in Biblical Times*. N.p.: self-published, 1981.

Wertenberger, Kathryn. "Bead Leno." *Handwoven*, March/April 1987.

Wilson, Kax. *A History of Textiles*. Boulder, CO: Westview Press, 1979.

2. Pick Up Leno

Best, Eleanor. *Lace by Hand*. N.p.: self-published, 2005.

Egen, Su. "Finnish Lace." *Handwoven*, March/April 1986.

Frey, Berta. *Seven Projects in Rosepath*. Saugerties, NY: self-published, 1948.

Moes, Dini. "Double Weave Duo." *Shuttle Spindle & Dyepot*, Winter 1994–1995.

Patrick, Jane. "Finger Control." *Handwoven*, March/April 1983.

Tidball, Harriet. *Two-Harness Textiles: The Open-Work Weaves*. Shuttle Craft Guild Monograph 21. Santa Ana, CA: HTH Publishers, 1967.

Wallace, Meg. "Pick-Up Leno." *The Weaver's Journal*, October 1976.

3. Bead Leno

Albert, Marvelyn. "A Knitted Look for Scarves." *Handwoven*. September/October 2006.

Alderman, Sharon. "Loom Controlled Leno." *Handwoven*, May 1981.

Atwater, Mary. "The Bead-Leno Weave." In *Practical Weaving Suggestions*, vol XI. Shelby, NC: Lily Mills, 1950.

Reeves, Martha. "Bead Leno, A Fabric for Garments." *Shuttle Spindle & Dyepot*, Summer 2011.

———. "My Magical COE Journey." *Shuttle Spindle & Dyepot*, Winter 2010–2011.

Sullivan, Donna. "Weaver's Primer." *Weaver's*, no. 15, 1991.

4. Pattern Techniques in Bead Leno

DeRuiter, Erica. "A Three-Shaft Scarf." *Handwoven*, May/June 2003.

Hodge, William. "Old Friend, New Twist." *Weaver's*, no. 38, 1997.

Reeves, Martha. "Bead Leno, A Fabric for Garments." *Shuttle Spindle & Dyepot*, Summer 2011.

Wertenberger, Kathryn. "A New Twist on Bead Leno." *Handwoven*, November/December 1989.

5. Pushing the Limits of Bead Leno

Alderman, Sharon and Wertenberger, Kathryn. *Handwoven Tailormade*. Loveland, CO: Interweave Press, 1982.

Lyon, Linda. "Leno Vest." *Prairie Wool Companion*, Summer 1983.

Rowley, Elaine. "Slightly Left of Center Jacket." *Prairie Wool Companion*, Summer 1983.

Xenakis, Alex. "The Ultimate T-Shirt." *Prairie Wool Companion*, Summer 1983.

6. Tarascan Lace

Best, Eleanor. *Lace by Hand*. N.p.: self-published, 2005.

Frey, Berta. *Seven Projects in Rosepath*. Saugerties, NY: self-published, 1948.

Jenkins, Evelyn. "Tarascan Lace." *Handweaver & Craftsman*, Winter 1960.

Thabet, Micheline. "Tarascan Lace." *The Weaver's Journal*, Spring 1984.

Tidball, Harriet. *Two-Harness Textiles: The Open-Work Weaves*. Shuttle Craft Guild Monograph 21. Santa Ana, CA: HTH Publishers, 1967.

index

Norwegian lace blouse.
Courtesy of Eric Rice Photography.

Courtesy of Unique Images.

Martha Reeves fell in love with weaving over twenty-five years ago, and retired from her career as a computer analyst to weave full-time. In 2010 she was awarded the Handweaver's Guild of America Certificate of Excellence Level II: Master with a specialized study in bead leno, a technique of weaving intricate lace cloth. Now a recognized authority in her field, she is devoted to sharing the secrets of weaving leno lace with weavers through workshops, lectures, and publications.

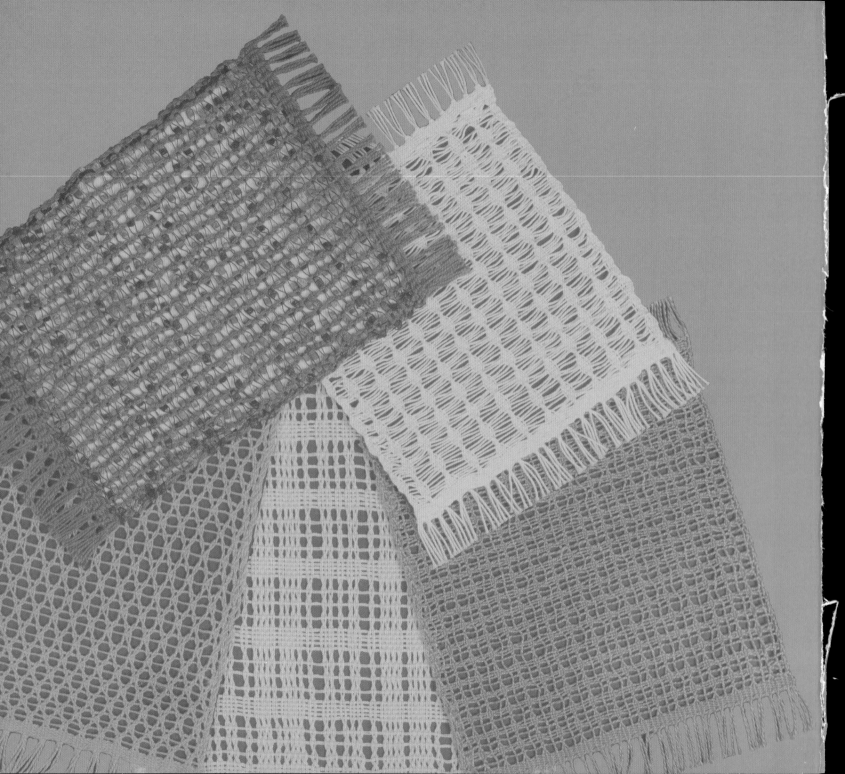